MAN-ERISMS

Being a Success in a

Masculine World

by Bethany Londyn

Bethany Londyn

Copyright Page

Publisher: ChickLit Media Group

ISBN 9781505266634

Disclaimer

Although the author and publisher have made every effort to ensure that the information in this book was acceptable at press time, they reserve the right to alter and update opinions expressed.

The material in this book is general opinions based on one person's view. It is not intended to be a substitute for professional or psychological advice. This book is for entertainment and empowerment purposes.

The author and publisher do not assume and hereby disclaim any liability to any party for any loss, damage, or disruption caused.

Acknowledgments

I dedicate this book to one of my best friends, Beth Willers, who encouraged me with her keen observations. Because of her, an opportunity was found to empower and inspire women all over the world.

I also want to acknowledge all the mothers, entrepreneurs, and hard-working women that excel past their assumed personal limitations and boundaries.

Love Period.

Free Resources

To enjoy the Free Resources provided with this book from Bethany Londyn, please see the exclusive Man-Erisms page on Londyn's site under MAN-ERISMS FREE RESOURCES.

http://www.bethanylondyn.com

CONTENTS

Bethany Londyn

Reasons to Read this Book

Interested in Simple Tips to Create a Shift in Your Job.

Learn what it might take to Lead Others.

Curious as to why you are still Sitting in the same Position for Years.

Remove confusion as to why Men have the Executive positions in your Company.

Figure out How Others Perceive You.

It's Time for a Change in Your Life

INTRODUCTION

First and foremost, I want to thank you for downloading the book, *"Man-Erisms."*

When my good friend, Beth Willers, sent me an email with all these points that she had been stockpiling based upon observations regarding how men operate in business and how she was starting to incorporate them to move forward in her position, I had no idea it'd eventually come this far! After reading through her list, I told her I was going to call it the "Bible in Business for Women." I referred to it almost every week and finally decided there was no way I could hold it back from other women, as I saw so much value in it. So we ended up writing an article about it, which received some great feedback, and now here I am turning it into a book!

As titled, this book intends to disrupt the current perception of women and how they interact in the workplace through unleashing value and worth. Many of these aspects are universal standards that men take on in their daily practice without even thinking about it. A real force to be reckoned with is when a woman uncovers their masculine side and combines it with their beautiful feminine side. One could also compare this to the balance of the Yin and Yang energy in Feng Shui.

This book contains steps and strategies on how embracing those masculine qualities can assist with climbing the ladder in your company, excelling as an entrepreneur, supporting salary increases, substantial, meaningful relationships, and living a fruitful life in general.

Great news shows an upswing in the shift of women in the workplace from assistants to executives and an increase in women-owned businesses. They have more than doubled in just shy of a decade. So how is it that these women are making it all happen? Well, maybe they are embracing their male counterpart's actions to get what they want. Here in this book, are some simple "Man-erisms" that you can follow to assist in your progression in the workplace.

Now is the time to take charge of your life, with simple action steps, so that you can achieve, as you deserve the best life experience possible! May this help you own the drive, confidence, knowledge, and strength that I know you already possess, which may need a little unlocking.

I want to preface that this book is not about changing who you are but merely guiding you towards the path of least resistance to get you where you want to go via some simple tips. It's time to shift, possibly get uncomfortable, and breakthrough to step into your power. By showing what men do and do not do in the workplace, it is also a hope that you reach greater heights in your business and the rat race that is the work setting.

Thanks again for purchasing this book. I hope you enjoy it!

CHAPTER 1

Do Not Apologize Unnecessarily

Unless you have done something seriously wrong, then you should never apologize as it subconsciously can be interpreted as a sign of weakness. Women tend to start sentences off with "I'm sorry" way too often, which is something that men rarely do. Men would never apologize when it is unwarranted, and neither should you.

According to Judi Clements of the Judi Clements Training & Development center, women are genetically inclined to be harmonious and nurturing. For women, apologizing is the best way to create a peaceful atmosphere and avoid tension between people. In an article in Bloomberg Business, researchers say that unneeded apologies give the "harm-doer" the power over the situation by handing over the controls. Withholding an apology doesn't necessarily mean admitting when you've done something wrong; it is a way of holding the upper hand via an acknowledgment. Author, Dr. Linda Sapadin of the self-help book "Master Your Fears: How to Triumph over Your Worries and Get on with Your Life," states it beautifully: "By taking responsibility for things that aren't your fault, you denigrate your self-esteem." You should never apologize just for the sake of avoiding confrontations; if you do, then people will treat you like a doormat and regularly step on you.

Let's paint a picture here. Say you are in the boardroom with your colleagues and a few of the bosses in your company. After presenting a very brilliant idea, you notice that the people inside the room are just looking at you, maybe a few blank stares, and some even decide to question your work and thoughts. Immediately, for some reason, you suddenly apologize to everyone because you thought that they didn't like your presentation or because you felt that the way you presented it was too forceful or too weak. This seemingly innocent act will make them reconsider accepting your work, what they would think is that you have no conviction of your presentation, and someone else may do a better job – and you would not want that to happen, right?

Another aspect is that women, by nature, are very commonly ruled by their emotions, and that's why words can easily take effect on them. Now that can be okay on a personal level, but when it comes to business and the workplace, keep emotions at bay. Women also tend to counteract, which not only discredits them but, depending on the type of reaction, sometimes leads them to the title of "bossy." When someone makes a comment that is aggravating in any way, it is essential to take a deep breath before responding. Some may think that by counter-reacting, they are using their voice as a form of leadership, however, although it's a necessity to be vocal, reacting could also lead to a situation where backtracking is then needed or even an apology. If backtracking to cover up what was said or done is the case, one will typically let the situation linger in their heads about what was said before deciding on how to deal with it. Unfortunately, just the act of thinking about what to do takes away from efficiency and productivity, as well.

On another note, when you consistently apologize often to a subordinate, an employee, or a colleague for raising your voice when issuing an order or request, it will show them that you hold yourself small and can easily be pushed around and taken for granted. When coming from a place of "small" and not owning what you say, for example, others will continuously think less of you and not take you seriously, which leads to less passion from your team and potentially even slacking off and less productivity of course.

Don't get the wrong idea, apologizing for when you are at fault is taking the upper hand. However, as mentioned previously, apologize when you've made a mistake; if you are not able to do this simple deed, then you are unreasonable. It is not worth it to be in a situation of apologizing for being "reactive" or even "bossy," funny as it technically maybe your job in the first place.

CHAPTER 2

Respect Yourself

Men (or at least real men) would not demean or belittle themselves in front of other people. To be treated like the professional that you are, then you better learn to treat yourself with the utmost respect as well.

People who demean themselves do not present themselves as leaders. So, if you are not a leader, then you are merely a follower, is this where you want to be? You must respect and own what you deliver. I know Mahatma Gandhi speaks of leadership through this quote, "There they go, and I must follow them, for I am their leader." However, part of the following is understanding your team's personalities and qualities to put them into a cohesive unit so that it is the most proficient, productive, and dominant team possible. However, if your goal is to follow and not lead others, then what is your intent in reading this book? Why are you even trying to climb the corporate ladder owning this kind of attitude? If you have no intention or drive for leading, then continue to confine yourself to the lonely cubicle for the rest of a rather bland career.

But, since you are reading this, then you must have some inkling of desire to get ahead of the rat race and be an influential leader for a change. By the way, a leader creates other leaders. So if you want to earn the respect of your fellow workers and make them want to follow you and be inspired, then you need to cut yourself some slack and stop belittling yourself. Keep your head up high and be proud of yourself and your skills and talents.

Real men have an unshakeable spirit that will not just accept any form of insult and mockery. If you want to become a good leader in the workplace, then you should embody this spirit yourself and start by being proud of all you have to offer.

Next time you think something negative about yourself, whether it is work-related or not, STOP and say something positive that you love. An example might be how something doesn't fit because you aren't getting to the gym, or how Ms. Roberts has it so much easier than you. STOP, and flip to something effortless that you believe about yourself, such as "I have the most amazing eyes." Slowly over time, you will start to notice a more positive version of yourself.

Another tactic to acquire is to journal every morning about how awesome you are, and why your company couldn't live without you.

Simple examples:

- I have a college degree
- I am a great listener
- I take direction well
- I care about my co-workers
- I am a fast learner

What did you put on your resume in the first place anyway? You had to put something positive to sell your worth to them, right?! Start living like it's the first week of a new job. Remember how you wanted to prove yourself? Show them why you are so valuable because you are. Rinse and repeat. Keep writing about why you are so fabulous.

If you feel any differently, it's time to go back to the drawing board, and start with the small things, such as "I love my eyes and the way they shine in the sunlight." You can expand from there, but there is no reason to do this only for a week, writing positive attributes, or even love letters can work wonders for you and your soul.

Then write down items of value that you did the day before to support somebody else. Giving to others always helps your worth as well. For example:

- I listened to Sergio for 30 minutes, as he vented about his day
- I supported David with his website by providing information on personal branding
- I helped Christy with office applications that assist in organizing her day

After doing this awhile, you will start looking for opportunities to assist others. You can also transfer to relationships, of course. Your relationships, friends, and family deserve to have you in their lives. Try these techniques for 45 days and see what starts to transpire.

When it comes to salary negotiations and raises, one must know their worth otherwise, why would your employer? I was talking to my friend the other day that owns a $50.0M company. He flat out told me he typically has women in the management positions because it mainly saves him money. If he promotes a guy, they will ask for a massive jump in salary right off the bat, sometimes along the lines of a 30-40% increase while doing less work. When he promotes a woman, they usually accept a small raise and ASK to prove their worth over three to six months before wanting to receive an assessment for an increase. For the men at this point, the financial raise is rarely around the amount asked for before also starting their new position.

The bottom line is to know your worth, know the value of the position that you want, and go for it. Don't be afraid to ask for a raise, either. Men sure have no fear. If you don't know your worth, start with the simple tasks above, and do some research by looking at other similar open positions that are commensurate with what you would be doing, maybe go online and check out salaries for similar jobs.

CHAPTER 3

"Own" Your Statements

Instead of saying, "I think..." you should own the statement. If you catch yourself starting a sentence with "I think that..." immediately change it to "Actually, I know that..." The above statement shows that you are unsure about your ideas while the latter allows you to claim knowledge. It may be reasonable for women to use "I think" because women consider many aspects, and they would rarely adapt a linear method of thinking. Men, however, have no qualms deciding firmly.

When you use non-committal statements, it leaves room for doubt; and when there's even a shadow of a doubt, your colleagues, subordinates, or even your bosses can and will notice it and immediately think that you are unconfident with your ideas. It is like you are giving people permission to step on your concepts and replace them with a statement of their own. To your boss, this also may sound like you are not ready, or that you slacked off and forgot something along the way. To your subordinates, this may show how you are on the same level as them and may result in them not treating you as respectfully.

Since you will be going against your natural predisposition, you need to make sure that you are 100% confident about your facts so you can avoid uttering non-committal statements because of any doubts. One thing you can do is to list the pros and cons of different ideas and tally the results, and then calculate the total scores. When you get ideas that seem to have more disadvantages then pros, you need to eliminate them right away.

To make things more transparent, here is an example. Say you are to present your bosses and co-workers your ideas about an upcoming project, and being a natural indecisive thinker, you still cannot decide what approach you need to show: so you have choices 1, 2, and 3. Since you only get to choose one, because of the limited time you have, first list the side of your choice by the side and think of their pros and con and tally them on your list.

1 2 3

Pros | Cons Pros | Cons Pros | Cons

x x x

x x x

x x x

Result:

DECISION 1 – Pros 2, Cons 1

DECISION 2 and 3 – Pros 1, Cons 2

Since 2 and 3 have two cons and one pro, as opposed to 1 with two advantages and one disadvantage, it is safe to say that you should choose to go with Choice #1. Having a firm conviction is better than merely saying, "I think we can go with decision 1, but there is also a chance for decision 2 to work; however, there's also some room for decision 3."

Men love bullet points anyways, whether it's how we speak, or even with emails. There's no need to add all the extra fluff. Just streamline thoughts that are clear and to the point.

If you are still having a hard time adapting to a linear way of thinking, you can also turn to your gut feeling to support the facts you've collected. What's important is that you commit to your statements or decisions without any wavering.

CHAPTER 4

Don't Be a Know-It-All

Well, many of us know that most women need to be right all the time. Don't get upset, you know it's true! This need makes women look like a know-it-all. Please, spare your co-workers from this kind of attitude.

You are not a teacher; you are leading a group of people. It is okay to claim statements and show confidence in yourself as discussed in earlier chapters, but if you are doing it just because you want to prove to yourself and to other people that you are right; or if you are doing it just so you can say "I told you so" later on, then forget about it. That's being obnoxious.

You will only push people away if you keep acting like a know-it-all. Do not get the wrong idea; make it clear to your co-workers that you know enough to be included in meetings and decision making. It is alright to be confident, but do not be overly self-assured. Find a balance between being submissive and the know-it-all character. Practice always makes perfect. As advised by Social Psychologist Amy Cuddy, "Fake it until you become it."

You should always step up to the plate and show people what you know. Especially when it is needed or when it will benefit the company; however, do not assume that your ideas are the only ones that matter. Doing so will show people that you are not willing to consider their opinions and that their thoughts are not worthy of even being discussed. With this kind of attitude, your relationship with your colleagues can turn sour. Even though you are a leader, you should also be a team player, as this fosters respect among your coworkers.

From another angle, it is safe to say that not everything you know is right; not everything you know is relevant, and not everything you know will benefit the company or the people in it. Always remember that what you feel is right, many times, translates differently to others, as people perceive and interpret what you say based on their attributions and stories. For example, where you see the white paper, someone might have glasses on with a green tint, so they will only see the green paper.

Before going and blurting out all the ideas stuck in your head, please stop yourself thinking differently this time. If you need to, make an imaginary filing cabinet in your head, sort the ideas you've collected so far, and file them appropriately. Take out only what is relevant, what is needed, and what is helpful. This way, you can still share your ideas without getting tagged as "Lil' miss know-it-all."

CHAPTER 5

Be an Imposing Figure

Amy Cuddy's research, as shown on a particular TED Talks episode, explained why knowing how to "Power Pose" is a solid action to practice in the workplace. The pose affects testosterone and cortisol level, making it a detrimental gear in achieving success.

Folding your arms, hunching over, and crossing your legs all makes women appear smaller. It forces us to take up less space. Unfortunately, many women have a negative perception of their body anyway, so all they want to do is cover it up, hide, or visually become smaller. These acts are done in many cases, subconsciously as well. You've probably heard the message, "actions speak louder than words."

Start taking up more space by standing up straight and widening your shoulders. Stop coming from a place of wanting to be small, as this will not serve you. Men love to take up as much of the space around them as possible by throwing their arms around in the air as they talk, walking around as they speak, and placing arms on the table. These actions are worthy of respect and are how they "dominate" their space.

Others will govern your space if you don't, which automatically will give them the upper hand. The one who seems to occupy the whole room just by his or her mere presence is the boss; the rest who position themselves on the sidelines are the inferior ones. A small gesture like standing tall with your chin up can exude an aura of authority. As you consume more space around you, others may start to back down and become more acquiescent.

I've seen women scoff at men's confidence. Men always seem so sure of themselves. What you may not know is that it is an innate survival strategy that shows other men that they are not to be stepped on. That is why most men end up at the top of the ladder or at least retain their cozy spot near the top. I advise you to start doing the same.

Consider these scenarios:

In a meeting, people want to pitch their ideas in the hopes of getting noticed by the top brass. When you are much too kind and accommodating by giving other people space, or you become swallowed by others pitching ideas alongside you, notice that you might sit there with your arms crossed and holding your thoughts back, which ultimately takes away confidence in your beliefs. Your holding back enables your co-workers to continue voicing their opinions, and when you leave the meeting frustrated. Eventually, you might gather your thoughts and email them out to everyone. At this point, you are not in a very suitable position. You must prove yourself to be an Alpha, or critical player if you want your ideas to not only be heard but potentially be the winning candidate. Utilizing the space around you sets you up for delivering from the point of power. Taking up more space sets the tone that you are at par, if not above your competition.

Sounds easy? Not really. The workplace is full of men who have mastered this art because it is their instinctual nature. Owning the space may not be easy if you are generally like a doormat or coming from a place of lack. Similar to always being stepped on without putting up much of a fight. These statements may seem harsh, yet it's only an awareness level that you may or not agree with for yourself.

Women also tend to be cautious of men because of their build and lowered powerful voices. Baby steps are ok, start with small gestures, and see what confidence starts to exude as you begin to dominate and own the space around you.

CHAPTER 6

Dress in Excellence

When you dress impeccably, you will feel like nothing can stop you. If you want your co-workers to respect you, then you should at least look the part. Don't play or twirl with your hair, lick your lips, and other things when you are in a meeting; you will lose credibility. Also, by acting indecently, you will not be seen as a force to be reckoned with in the workplace. Trust me.

Do not dress up in miniskirts, short shorts, and blouses with plunging necklines if you want people to take you seriously. Dressing in this manner will only make your male counterparts think of you like a certain kind of woman — someone that they are interested in temporarily, not one that is valued and respected. As mentioned repeatedly in this book, if you want people to respect you, then you have to respect yourself first. Baring too much skin in the office will get you to all the wrong places, which also makes people look down on you or not take you seriously. If you don't want to be the kind of woman people gossip about, have enough self-dignity to dress respectably, and act appropriately.

As discussed in the previous Chapter, creating space can be hard for women because of their physiques. Knowing this information, it is essential to add additional prestige by allowing your clothing to represent your worth and do some talking for you.

Appropriate dressing goes hand in hand with how you should act. Wear clothes that mean business. Make full use of colors, structures, and the like; clothes that are not of excellent quality and fit show that you do not take yourself seriously because you did not even take the time to dress well. Wear your power. Act not based on your gender, but on your greatness as a member of the company that deems ownership.

CHAPTER 7

Do Not Ask, Tell

Let's say there is a situation where you need to get off early one day to go to the doctor or pick up the kids from school. Whatever the case is, women typically go into an elaborate story of why they need to get off work early or come in late. They go into all the details; for example, my nanny is sick, the car broke down, whatever the story or excuse is they spell it all out. When a guy needs to leave early, they may say, I'm going to leave at 4p today. He doesn't state I'm going to leave earlier because I need to do this and that. He may say when he's coming back. Regardless, it's just that simple, no explanation required, and so powerful. If the boss needs an account of what's happening, they will ask for it. Still, though, don't elaborate, be black and white. "I need to leave early to pick up my kid." That is all that is necessary.

Looking deeper into questioning, know that there is always a time and place. It is reasonable to ask questions when you do not understand something; there are even times when asking is commendable. It can show humility and your eagerness to learn. On the other hand, too much asking can mean you do not know a thing about the industry or the business you are in - almost like you can't learn on your own. Asking too many questions can also make you look like you are allowing the other person to decide for you instead of listening to yourself and owning your voice.

Statistics show that 72% of men believe that women ask too

many questions. Likewise, 80% of women admit that they prefer to ask questions, even when they know the answer. In an article written for Forbes magazine, famous authors Barbara Anis and John Gray, co-authors of the book "Work With Me: The Eight Blind Spots Between Men and Women in Business", claim that their findings show that women ask questions not just to get answers, but also to build consensus with others, show concern for a project or others, to offer feedback, and to ask for support. That is admirable in that sense.

Now, while it is true that asking questions may help in reaching a point of consensus as the thoughts of the majority go into consideration, it can also show that you don't possess the right leadership traits that will enable you to come up with a singular decision for the group. It can mean one of two things: either you can't stand up for your thoughts, or you cannot come up with your own decision.

Even in regular conversations at work, or when you are speaking with your boss, it can be impressive when you suddenly say a fact that's interesting and relevant to the conversation or a new marketing strategy that you feel can apply to your company's efforts. You should never stop trying to learn new things. Stay attuned to the nature of your industry, as it helps to be in the know at all times. Of course, to gain all of the knowledge that you need, you must ask the right kinds of questions. Look into their opinions on the subject or offer thoughts on matters regarding the information that they might have.

There are times when asking a question is appropriate, but asking too many will only annoy the people that you work with. Find the right balance between asking questions and voicing out your answers.

CHAPTER 8

Don't Let Them See You Cry

It is a well-known fact that women tend to be more emotional than men, or rather, they tend to let their emotions show. Thank you, hormones! Men, on the other hand, rarely allow their feelings to show, and they would also never have their feelings get the best of them. Master your feelings if you want to become an effective leader in your workplace.

From another angle, because women can be so in tune with their emotions, as they are compassionate by nature, this allows them to understand and read the feelings of others, which is most definitely an advantage. Empathizing with your co-workers creates a space to share ideas and work as a cohesive unit. The key, however, is to notice the feelings, but not let emotions take control because then you are in for a world of trouble.

Picture this: you just got called out by your immediate superior for a simple mistake that is not even entirely your fault. Now, because you're quite emotional, you cannot help but tear up, cry, or react in plain sight of your team as you got so worked up. Yikes, this is not good. Not only does your team see that you are not the type of person who can handle pressure well, but that you are also weak when antagonized by someone else. In turn, you may lose admiration from people working around you, furthermore under you. The messages can signal others to take advantage and potentially try to claim your job or the position you are after.

This is not to say that you have to keep your emotions bottled up inside of you; it is quite ok to release them, just not in front of your co-workers. Pause, take a deep breath, or two or three, and take a walk outside for a moment to shake it off. Your emotions can be a powerful tool when used correctly, but they are also a double-edged sword that can harm you if you are careless enough to lose control. Do not show them any sign of weakness, as it provides others an opportunity to overtake you in the workplace.

CHAPTER 9

Be a Person of Few Words

Learning how to express your ideas in as few words as possible is extremely powerful. Do not lead your co-workers on and on with your ramblings and story after story. After a couple of minutes, they will slowly tune you out and not even listen to what you have to say. The attention span of most people is not that long, so you need to make do with what little amount of time you have and get your point across immediately. As previously discussed in Chapter 3, men love bullet points.

Women, by nature, are quite talkative; they like to try to explain every little detail regarding their ideas to whoever feels like listening to them. Men, on the other hand, tend to summarize their thoughts and share them using the minimum amount of words. This is the commonly looked upon reason women are seen as naggers who talk non-stop.

Plain and simple, do not mince your words, and do not sugarcoat everything that you want to say. If you are the bringer of bad news to your team, do not beat around the bush; tell them straight out what they need to hear. If one of your team members is not performing as he should, tell him directly, preferably in private. By all means, do not use passive-aggressive behavior in the hopes that one will get your message eventually; it will only spark unnecessary confusion and possibly confrontation as well.

If you want to act like a man in your workplace, then you should learn how to talk like one. Get to the point immediately, and if possible, do not make a long-winded speech about it; you only have a few minutes wherein you have your audience's full attention, so make sure you make the best out of it.

If you have ever seen any of the Godfather movies, you will see how powerful a moment of silence is. Don Vito Corleone, the Godfather, can send a message to his underlings without saying a word. It is like his stares are enough for people to get the information. A stance and stare are the kind of skills that you should learn because sometimes silence can say more than a thousand words.

Let's say you are in negotiations for something, whether it be selling an idea, or even making a powerful statement during a presentation, always embrace the uncomfortable silence. If you are face to face, gauge the facial expressions before you speak so that powerful statements and questions get to land for them during the silence. Also, usually, this silence is much shorter than it feels like. If on the phone, simply pause. Then you could ask something like, "Does that make sense??"

If you have to stay silent until they break the silence, here's an example: "You asked me for $50,000, and I offered you $40,000." Your answer could be, "Well, I am willing to negotiate a small amount, but $40,000 is not an option." Then let there be silence. Have them come back to you if they are trying to play hardball. I know this can be scary, but do not give in!!! If someone is not willing to pay what you are worth, why do you want to subject yourself to them in the first place? Know your worth.

CHAPTER 10

Steer Clear of Personal Information

Steer clear of personal information. Similar to being in court, or pulled over by a cop. As mentioned previously, less is always more. What you say can be used against you. Don't share personal information unless explicitly asked. It's none of their business. Rarely do men talk about their own lives in the workplace. I notice all the time that men are digging into women and interrogating them. Beware of this tactic; they can and will use it against you when you least expect it. Next thing you know, they will call you out on your productivity because they know you just broke up with your boyfriend or some other story that you've leaked.

Let's take this out to the social atmosphere now. Be careful with co-workers and employee relationships as friends and hanging out after hours. I'm all about creating a workplace community and culture, similar to companies such as NIKE and Zappos. Once again, though, you still want to be careful about personal info shared. If you tell someone about how your best friend is taking advantage of you by staying at your house longer than expected, next thing you know, they are calling you out during the day because you aren't as effective or productive as usual because they know you are having home-related issues.

Be warned of after-work drinks too. I believe connecting with people is essential; however, keep your alcohol to a minimum. Drinking with others rarely leads to anything good. It also provides another substantial opportunity to dive into your personal life.

It truly is a climb to the top in some businesses, and being aware of this is crucial. There are many cases of people "pretending" to be your friends just to get more information from you. It's pretty disgustingly unethical to me, but regardless, it's about getting ahead regardless of what it looks like. Manipulation runs rampant in many aspects of our lives, so it's material to take note and become aware of situations where this is taking place. Recognition is the first step!

If anything, be the one asking questions rather than being the one giving the answers. This is a perfect play on being the one in control of the conversation. Have you ever noticed that certain people usually ask all the questions? Then you try and change the conversation, but then they retake control? Be that the one controlling the conversation. Most people love talking about themselves anyways, right? Why not be the listener and learn? And when you listen, really listen, you may find an opportunity to be of support such as mentioned in Chapter 2.

CHAPTER 11

Always Be Prepared

A man is always ready for whatever comes his way, and you should be too.

There is a joke about how it takes forever for a woman to get ready when going out. That should not be the case when you are in the workplace. You need to prepare in case something unexpected comes up, and you have to work out a solution immediately. Most women would start panicking and let their emotions run all over the place, which is not what you want to happen for obvious reasons. So you should take a page out of the Boy Scouts' manual and always be prepared.

The 10 Second Speech

One of the things that you should have with you at all times is a 10-second speech that introduces yourself and tells about your position and responsibilities in the company. You never know when you will be sharing an elevator ride with the top executives of your company, so having a 10-second speech prepared to introduce yourself professionally and make a lasting impression during an extremely short trip to the top can be priceless.

As mentioned again and again throughout this book, you should get your message across using as few words as possible. When you bump into someone of influence, complimenting their tie or choice of shoes is nice; however, everyone can do it, and most likely, it will not make a standing impression of precisely who you are and why you are worthy of them knowing you. Acknowledge them, introduce yourself, and make sure that you can impress them using just a sentence or two.

For instance, you can start by stating your name and job title, then immediately segue into your most recent accomplishments, like how you were able to increase the productivity of your department by convincing your supervisor to switch to a new and software program. You should never let yourself get caught with your pants down, so be ready to strike whenever the opportunity presents itself. If you want to make waves, then you should always be prepared to set yourself up for a win with a stand out first impression when the time is right by reacting in a strong, professional manner. Or maybe you are out at a social function and meeting others. Honestly, you just never know who you might run into, and you want to deliver a clear picture of who you are and what you have to offer.

For example, "I'm Bethany Londyn, CEO of ShopAddiKt.com, a valuable fashion resource sourcing various lifestyle verticals for consumers, as well as providing strong data trends for brands and retailers." Boom. One hears this, and they think, "Hmmm interesting, I want to know more." Or they don't, and that's just fine as well. If one isn't interested in what I have to say, it might not be the right person to be talking to, but I sure can listen to them, connect, and see what they are all about as well.

CHAPTER 12

Continuing to Claim

Your Power

In this chapter, I want to talk about multiple situations where you get to own your self-worth, your beliefs, and standing as a source for the opportunity.

First off, you must always be learning. When you understand your industry and what's going on in the world, above the surface, it adds to your value. You will be able to talk the talk which can open more doors and get you where you want today. Knowledge truly is power; this isn't the first time you have heard this. And as discussed previously, do not hold back your voice and opinions. People have no idea what they are missing if you do not express your thoughts and own them. It is a disservice to hold back in many cases.

Another thing to be aware of is speaking fast. When you breathe and speak at the same time, it comes out slower and powerful. Talking excited and fast can be a woman's nature, but it doesn't necessarily serve us when delivering something important or a powerful statement.

When it comes to the contract for the job or anything you have to sign really, do not show fear by immediately signing. Asking for edits shows your power. I mean, you are putting your money, reputation, etc. on the line. You get to be happy and comfortable with it, so the contract gets to be just right. Don't be afraid of what it looks like to them. If the situation was flipped, would they be asking for changes? Most likely, the answer is yes. Never sign anything you do not feel right about.

So, now, let's fast forward and say you have the job and the employees beneath you that you are leading. If there is an employee that you have tried to empower to their greatness, yet is still not cutting the mustard, do not be afraid to let them go. For some people making people go can be easy, but for many, it's not. Women and our beautiful, compassionate motherly sides take over, and we feel terrible about letting someone go because they may have kids, or whatever the story might be. Remember, though; it's not about how much you "like" someone. They wouldn't necessarily take the stand for you if the situation was flipped anyways! So, if they are not performing and executing the job as necessary, they get to go.

Also, think back to a time when either you or someone you know was let go or fired. Was it horrible for them? Yes, probably, for a short time, but from any situation, I can think about, it also empowered them to shift, almost like a big kick in the pants. Within months the individual was on to bigger and better things. Know when someone is let go, of course assuming it falls within all HR regulations, that although it can be detrimental to their life for a short time, you are not only doing a favor for the company, but for them as well. It creates a sense of urgency and holds the person accountable to learn from the situation and potentially create a better opportunity for themselves.

CHAPTER 13

Live in Acknowledgement
and Gratitude

Now, this is the only chapter that isn't about embracing the men's qualities. It's purely about being an amazing, joyful, loving individual. We get to embrace our feminine, supportive, and compassionate qualities as a potent edge and final touch to living a fruitful life and the best work-life experience possible.

Ending the day with a gratitude journal is extremely powerful. It not only shows you how blessed you are, but it also sets the tone to live a joyous life from a state of appreciation. Living from a state of satisfaction releases stress, anxiety, and unnecessary frustrations. Living in gratitude puts us in the present, and that's just the place you want to live from to be in the Zen and the most relaxed.

Then you can take this one extra step and start to acknowledge others. How well does it feel when someone recognizes your hard work? Or something that inspired you? It could be as something such as "I want you to know that you inspired me today to wear something out of the norm, for me, and I love it" or "I want to acknowledge what you said to Mr. Carey yesterday. That was great feedback, and it empowered me to do the same with someone else." People love affirmations, and it also is a way to show that you are grateful for them as well. If someone does something meaningful for you, don't be afraid to share that with them.

Sometimes face to face can be uncomfortable, and that can be something for you to work on, but in the meantime, you can write a simple note and pop it in the mail. Notes and Thanks You's mean the world to people. Emails are not what I'm saying here. Everyone gets enough of those. Be brave and courageous, and tell someone to thank you or give them acknowledgment. This shows not only that you are paying attention, but it also sets the tone for that person to receive from you. Your energy can be powerful alone. Try it for 45 days and see what happens, my guess is you will choose to do this for life.

CONCLUSION

I hope this book brought some thoughts for you up to the surface and enlightened you with some simple tips for how you choose to act in business. Although these are my opinions, I intend for them to shift your perception and encourage excellence and greatness in all areas of your life.

Finally, if you enjoyed this book, please take the time to share your thoughts and post a review on Amazon and GoodReads. It'd be much appreciated!

If you are curious to know more, Bethany Londyn has been putting regular content out on YouTube, Instagram, & more. Follow her or check out her website BethanyLondyn.com to stay current!

Thank you, and cheers to your dreams!

ABOUT THE AUTHOR

Bethany Londyn has spent over a decade in entrepreneurial-based Management & Sales positions within the Finance and Real Estate sectors, built up a Real Estate Portfolio, and taken part in a couple of startups over the past few years. She increased market share at her companies by creating strategic marketing plans and business relationships. Londyn holds a Bachelor of Science in Business Finance from Portland State University.

Londyn has her consulting firm: Londyn Heights LLC, under which she supports what she is most passionate about startups and empowering others. Londyn also practices Spiritual Healing and Intuitive Personal Development coaching for individuals aspiring to reach a new level in their life. She is passionate about spreading the message so that everyone recognizes that they have the possibility of achieving their dreams.

You will find companies and CEO's hiring her when there are more significant decisions to be made, or when they need a little insight behind specific scenarios.

In her free time, Bethany creates art and stays active, participating in pretty much anything the great outdoors has to offer.

If you are curious to know more, Bethany Londyn has been putting regular content out on YouTube, Instagram, & more. Follow her, or check out her website BethanyLondyn.com to stay current!